Have You Ever Wanted to Die?

by
Frances Dupree

Dedication

This book is dedicated to my husband. I thank you for always supporting me and giving me your honest opinion. Thank you for loving the broken parts of me and being willing to help in my healing process.

To my sons, my young Kings, for loving me no matter what. The love you guys have given me has gotten me through many dark days. I love all of you endlessly and it is truly an honor and a blessing to be your mom.

To my one and only princess, you were definitely worth the wait.

To my mother-in-law, my mom, thank you for being my soundboard through many things. I thank God for you and now I truly understand the respect, love, and loyalty that Ruth had for Naomi.

To my dad, thank you for allowing me to learn from my life mistakes but always loving me and being an amazing grandpa.

To those who have wanted or wants to die, God has spared you because you are not only chosen, but you are called. You have a great assignment in your life and that is why the enemy has been attacking you so bad and trying to take you out. But God. Don't give up.

Your breakthrough is within arm's reach. I love you and God does too. You are so important and there is a need for you in the Kingdom.

Table of Contents

*"I shall not die, but live, and declare
the works of the Lord."*
Psalms 118:17

Introduction

There were many days in my life that I simply wanted to die. There have been many nights I prayed, cried, and begged God not to allow me to wake up. I didn't understand why I wasn't good enough to be loved. Why couldn't I be raised by my mom and dad? Why didn't they want me? Why didn't they love me? Why did God continue to take away everyone whom I build a close relationship with? How come He wouldn't simply allow me to die? Little did I know that there was a calling on my life. That the tests were building my testimony. That there would be souls waiting to be healed through me sharing my pain. So, through my wanting to die, God was preparing me for greatness.

I have accomplished the hardest thing in my life which was to **LIVE** and not die. Have you ever wanted to die? Let me share my story with you and when you're done reading, let me teach you also how to **LIVE** and not die.

Chapter 1
What Broke Me

Growing up I always felt that I wasn't good enough. I didn't grow up with my mom or my dad. I asked myself often how terrible could a child be that neither parent wanted them? How could a mom have a child and not want to fight with every fiber of her being to have her? How could a father have a baby girl, but never wants to see her? These thoughts haunted me for many years of my life even into adulthood.

When I was seven years old my mom bought me the newest Barbie doll house and car that came with it. I hated barbies. And even though, I kept telling her not to buy them for me, she kept buying them. So, to make my point those barbies had to burn. I put them in the fireplace and my mom beat me and I ran to my best friend's house. My mom would always tell me after she whooped me if I didn't like it, I could leave. Well, that day I didn't like it and I left. Little did I know this would be the last time that my little sister and I would live with our mom. Nor did I know this one event would destroy me for most of my life.

I vaguely remember riding in the back of the police car to the station. When I got there, they started asking me so many questions about my mom, sister, and my step-dad. They took pictures of every part of my body. I was embarrassed, the social worker told me not to worry, they were going to take me someplace safe. I felt a sense of relief when she said that but I didn't understand why. There are so many gaps in my childhood, especially the short time that I did live with my mom. I don't ever remember her being terrible, nor do I remember her hating me either. So, it's still a mystery to me as to why I felt relieved.

When my mom came to the police station the disgust and pain on her face I will never forget. They kept us separated the whole time. My sister was taken in the back and pictures were taken of her as well. After a few hours I heard my mom crying as she was leaving and that was heartbreaking, not because she was crying but because she said, "No they can't take my baby!" I remember thinking to myself, *What about me?*

The first foster home that we went to there was a wife and a husband. They didn't have any other children. They were so loving and if I didn't know any better, I would have thought they were my real mom and dad. It was the ideal family. The dad went to work and the mom was with us all day. She cooked for us, read us stories, played with us, and combed our hair. She was just so sweet and so loving, I wished that we could stay with them forever.

Sadly, this heaven-sent family didn't last long. I don't remember all the details but from what I do remember is that they couldn't afford to keep us. When they sat me down to tell me that soon we would be leaving. My heart broke. All I could think was I'm really unlovable that's why they are getting rid of us. They kept saying how much they loved us, but if they really loved us why send us away?

My mom contacted my sister's dad and his family to let them know what was going on. Next thing I knew there were talks of my sister going to live with her grandma. First, we had to leave this wonderful family and my sister was leaving me. We would have visits with our mom and I asked her if I was going to live with my grandma too? She told me no, that my dad didn't want nothing to do with me. This the first time I remember her telling me this.

When we got back to our foster home, I cried myself to sleep that night. First my mom cried as they were taking her baby, soon we were leaving the heaven-sent family's home, and then my sister's grandma was getting her. I thought to myself, *why is my sister lovable but not me?* The dreadful day finally came and I had to say goodbye to my sister. I don't think I ever cried that hard in my life. I loved her even though a little part of me hated her because she was loved and I wasn't. I didn't want her to go. I didn't want to be alone. How come I couldn't go?

.

Chapter 2
When the Enemy Crept In

When I left that foster home I went to other foster homes, but I don't remember them. The only thing about elementary school that I remember is that I used to walk over this long bridge in order to get to the other side. In junior high I remember being a part of the drill team but I can't tell you anything else beyond that. I have memories of going to court and playing with other kids while waiting to go in the courtroom.

For a while my mom was coming to court and I didn't understand at the time why I couldn't sit with her at the table. I wasn't allowed to talk to her until after they would let us visit for a while. Then a day came I was at court and my mom wasn't there. This started to be the routine of court from that point. She didn't show up anymore. *What did I do? Why didn't my mom want to fight for me anymore? Was I really that terrible?*

I was in a group home called Hollygrove. My mom would visit and I was always so excited to see her. I would hug her and cry when it was time for her to leave because I wanted to go home. But she would always say they said she is an unfit mother. I would talk to my granny almost every day. I had a lot of friends but after a while I stopped trying to make friends because they would eventually leave and I would still be there. My sister's aunt would visit me but I don't remember my sister coming. We did a lot of activities while I was there, went to Disneyland, Magic Mountain, and camp. So, I guess there were some good things on top of the bad. One Christmas I met Kobe Bryant and Shaq from the Lakers. They came and gave us gifts.

My mom would visit me often, but one dreadful day we were supposed to have our visit and I sat by the window all afternoon and she didn't show up. I remember calling granny crying and being so angry. *What did I do to her? Why didn't she want to see me?* It became the new norm; we would talk on the phone often but she wouldn't show up for our visits. My hurt turned into anger, and then rage. I remember walking down a hall throwing everything in sight and I flipped over this big fish tank. Poor fish didn't do anything wrong;

they were just in the wrong place at the wrong time.

I attempted to kill myself for the first time, honestly, I don't even remember how. I just know I was in Alhambra hospital, a mental hospital. They said I was depressed and I was put on Prozac and Paxil. To my surprise my mom visited me. *How did she find me? Maybe she did love me after all.* She made me catfish, homemade mac and cheese and greens with cornbread which were my favorite foods at the time. I was so heartbroken when she left because I was ready to go home. That was the first and the last time that she visited me in the mental hospital.

I stayed there for a while because I wasn't cooperating. I didn't want to talk in group. Sometimes I had to be held down in order for my meds to be shoved down my throat. I tried to cut myself while I was there and I was tied down to a bed. The one good thing that I remember is the pool. I loved to swim, but the crazy part is I don't remember when I was taught. It was very relaxing for me though. I would swim as many laps as I could until the staff would tell me that I had to get out.

I eventually got my act together and I was able to return to the group home. When I realized my mom wasn't going to be showing up for visits the hurt started to hurt less. I stopped being devastated. At some point in time, I just made up in my mind that she was never going to come so I didn't even look for her anymore. The crazy part was that we talked on the phone often. Honestly, I can't really recall a time when we didn't talk on the phone.

To this day I never understood why she could talk to me regularly on the phone but she couldn't visit me. As I grew up, I learned that it's not that easy to face your mistakes. Everyone can't handle taking responsibility for their wrong, especially not being able to look your daughter in the face and say I failed you. It wasn't until many years later that I had a daughter of my own, my mom explained it all to me.

Chapter 3
This is Really My Reality

I ended up going to another group home called Hathaway. This one was located on top of a hill. When I first got there, I pretty much stayed to myself. I didn't want to get attached to anyone because every time I built an attachment they would leave and I would feel that pain all over again. I could never understand why no one would stay. They were always leaving me.

One of the girls there was really good at doing hair. So, I asked her if she could wash my hair and braid my hair for me. I was never taught how to do my hair, someone else always did it, or I went to the shop. There was a set up almost like a shop. I got up in the chair and put my head back in the sink so she could wash my hair. As she was washing my hair, she put her hand in my shirt and started playing with my nipple. I knew in my mind that it was wrong but I didn't tell her to stop because I liked how it made me feel.

Then she started to suck my nipple. I still didn't say anything. *How could something you knew was absolutely wrong feels so good?* She heard someone coming down the hall and stopped. I never told anyone what happened because I was ashamed that I liked it. I also didn't know the lasting effects that it would leave on me.

The school that we went to was up on the mountain as well. We would walk across the grass through the bushes to get to school. We went to school with the boys on the other side of the group home and kids that were bused in. They either got kicked out of school or their foster parents requested for them to go.

I liked this boy named Josh. He was light skinned and had pretty eyes. We would write letters back and forth to each other because outside of school we weren't allowed to have contact. A few times we sneaked away and kissed each other, but that was the extent of our relationship. One day we were walking up to the school and everyone kept looking at me and whispering. I had no idea what was going on. Josh left a note on my desk breaking up with me because he wanted to date one of my housemates. I was so mad. *Why did he have to make such a big deal about it? So stupid,* I thought.

The girl that now became my hair stylist was leaving and going home to her grandma, all I kept thinking was who's going to do my hair now? I was also hoping she didn't tell anyone what happened between us. We stayed in contact and I ended up going to another foster home. The family was a blur. I don't remember anything about them. I do remember that they allowed me to go to my hairstylist's grandma's house so she could braid my hair.

I got some blonde extensions and when she was done with my hair, I immediately called my foster mom to tell her I was done. She told me that she was running errands and asked if it would be ok if I stayed until she was done. I asked the girl and she said yes. Next thing I knew she had her hand down my shirt again. *Why did I get so stiff? How come I wouldn't tell her no? But most importantly why did I like it?* She pulled my pants down and started to lick me between my legs and that felt even better. But I still felt stiff, unmovable and like a mute.

There was a knock at the door; it was her uncle letting us know that my ride was there. We acted as if nothing ever happened, but I never communicated with her again. I had written a letter to a friend of mine who lived at the group home and like a dummy, I told her everything that had happened. It was the staff's duty to read all the letters before giving them to the house mates. The letter never got to my friend, but a call was made to the girl's grandma and my foster family.

Chapter 4
The Truth Hurts

I was in high school and I tore a ligament in my ankle. My current foster mom worked at Kaiser and one day she came home and showed me a little piece of paper. This piece of paper had my dad's number, address, and date of birth on it. I called my mom throwing a big fuss and I lied and said that I needed surgery and the foster system wouldn't pay for it. After years of telling me she didn't know his number she gave me the number so fast and said don't tell him I told you.

I called him and he said hello and I hung up. I called back and he said hello and I hung up again. I called back and he said hello and this time he said if you hang up on me, I'm not answering. I chuckled a little and asked, "Do you know who this is?" He said, "Yes you're my daughter, I have been waiting on this call for fifteen years." I immediately broke down crying and tried to tell him everything but between the ugly cry I had to hand the phone over to my foster mom.

I ended up living with my dad. My foster mom was so good to me but I didn't want to live with her anymore, since I had met my dad. I wanted to live with him. I had a love/hate relationship towards him. My mom had told me my whole life that he didn't love me, didn't want to have anything to do with me and he would rather raise his brother then raise me. I hated him for that because all that time I spent in foster care and group homes; he could have saved me. All the times I thought no one loved me, he could have loved me.

I loved him because he was kind and sweet but very stern. I love him because I always wanted to know him and to meet him and for him to be proud of me. I learned later that the whole time my mom knew exactly where he was and he was giving her money for my clothes and shoes which I never got. I understood why she said don't tell him where I was and she was so angry when she found out I moved in with him.

I was heartbroken to my core for two reasons, one, my mom allowed me to suffer so she could get what she wanted from him. I didn't have to be in foster care and group homes. I didn't have to be in a mental hospital. All she had to do was call him. Second, my heart was broken because he never asked to see me, he figured when I was ready, I would find him. *Why wasn't I good enough for him to ask to see me to want me to want to have a relationship with me? What did I do that was so wrong that my mom allowed me to suffer and live with strangers so she can continue to get material things from my father? Why wasn't I good enough to love?*

My dad and I bumped heads so many times. I take full responsibility for that because I purposely went against everything he said. I loved him but I hated him all at the same time. I never gave him a real chance to build a relationship with me because I was so full of hurt, anger, and pain. He worked out of town so when I was going to school most of the time, he was asleep and when I was going to sleep, he was coming home.

One of my favorite memories with him is that he said I couldn't use the dishwasher. I had to wash the dishes by hand. Of course, I didn't listen so when he was at work, I would use the dishwasher but I would make sure to put the dishes away before he got home. I thought I was slick. Well, he taught me good. I came home one day and the whole dishwasher was gone. There was an empty spot under the sink where the dishwasher used to be. All I could do was laugh. We had a lot of good times but there were also a lot of bad.

Chapter 5
When I Loved but Hated

My attitude was that he didn't raise me and didn't want me, I was already raised and he couldn't change me. When I first met my uncle, nana, and aunt I was so in love. My aunt was like my best friend. For a summer I went to live with my Nana. My uncle and I are the same age, but his birthday is a few months before mine. So, in his mind I'm his little cousin and I'm supposed to do what he says. In my mind we were the same age and I didn't have to listen to him.

At first, we were so close, we went everywhere together and did everything together. But that soon changed because I didn't want to listen to him anymore. We would get into fist fights because I would purposely go against him. After so long it was too much for him to handle, I wasn't easy to deal with at all. He kept telling my Nana and one day she sent me back to my dad.

I felt like I had been thrown away. I was so hurt and I remember walking in the house to my dad crying. *Why did she just throw me away like that?* To be honest, I was a handful my nana, aunt, and uncle welcomed me with open arms. They did everything for me and gave me basically everything I wanted. But that resentment and hate always crept in because of my childhood. I was devastated but it was my fault.

Before I went to bed that night, I cut both of my wrists. I honestly don't remember how my dad found out. But he cried and he was so hurt that I did that to myself. He cleaned my wrist and bandaged them up. He told me he loved me and was scared he didn't really know what to do. He put me in therapy and tried to spend more time with me. But I just kept telling myself no one will ever truly love me. I just wanted to die.

One afternoon my dad told me to do something I don't remember what it was, but I talked back and I told him that I was going to leave. I walked towards the garage door and he drug me by my hair from the garage door to my room. After crying and throwing a huge fit in my room I called my social worker Mr. Dario and I told him what happened. He told me that he couldn't do anything because my dad had full custody of me and I was no longer a ward of the court.

I went to school the next day and I told the principal, my teachers, and my counselor. They called my dad and I don't know what he said to them but they didn't take me seriously. When I got home from school he was there and he told me they contacted him and as long as I lived with him, I had to follow his rules. If I ever left, I wouldn't be welcomed back. I went to school the next day and I never went back home to my dad. I went to live with my friend Allah she lived on an Indian reservation. I went to school every day but I didn't go home.

One day I knew he was at work and my great grandmother was home. Mother is what we all called her, I went to the house to try and get clothes and she told me that he told her I wasn't allowed in the house anymore. I was so angry; *how could he not allow me to just simply get my clothes?* I didn't really like Mother. Her and my dad was so close and I was jealous of their relationship. When she visited, she took over and it was her way, I didn't like it at all.

I remember one time I asked my Nana if she could take Mother somewhere so I could hang out with my dad without her. It was supposed to be a secret between my Nana and I. But my big mouth, my dad and I were talking and some kind of way I ended up telling him and he was so mad. He had some colorful words for me and my Nana. I never did that again but it just made me dislike her even more. I felt like just her presence turned him against me. Now here she was at the door not letting me in, I knew we didn't get along but I was wishing and hoping that she would be on my side for once but nope.

I was so spiteful I would mail letters and cards to my dad lying to him and saying that I was pregnant. Telling him such awful things. At the time I thought it was funny because I could picture him turning red, but now that I think about it, that was such a hateful thing to do. My dad wasn't a perfect man but I'm sure he didn't know how to be a father to a broken teenager like me. He didn't break me and it wasn't fair for me to expect him to know how to heal me.

Chapter 6
Finally, I'm Loved

My friend and I went to her boyfriend's house and that's when I first saw him, my first love. OMG he was so fine and a bad boy! My friend and her boyfriend went in the room and we were in the living room talking, laughing, and flirting with each other. I was so ratchet next thing you know I was sitting on his lap and we were kissing. Little did I know he would turn out to be my first love. Before my friend and I left we exchanged numbers.

I never met anyone like him before I kept thinking about him. We would text often on the phone. The dreadful day came and my friend's uncle said I couldn't stay anymore. Her grandma was really sick and having an extra mouth to feed had become more stress than she could handle. I was so sad because I didn't want to leave, honestly, I had nowhere to go. I couldn't go back to my dad's. So, I made a phone call that would change my life forever.

I called the fine bad boy and he came straight to my rescue. He picked me up and took me to stay with him and his family. They were so loving and welcoming but it was weird for me at first because I felt like a charity case even though they never treated me that way. Honestly it was as if I had a brand-new family overnight. They loved on me and the fine bad boy was amazing. He worked and took care of me and bought me everything that I needed.

He was my first and it was so natural and loving. He didn't pressure me in any way. I remember it like it was yesterday. We showered together and then we made love. The way he touched, kissed, and caressed me there was no way this was just sex. I was a little embarrassed because his mom was in the next room. But he held me all night after and something about that forehead kiss was everything. I instantly fell in love.

He was the first person in my life to show me pure and genuine love. Not only did he show me but his family did as well. For the first time in my life, I felt complete, like I belonged, and was finally good enough. I was actually worth being loved. I could be loved, maybe I was expecting it from all the wrong people.

I tried to transfer schools. I was a senior in high school but my dad wouldn't release my transcripts. Fine bad boy took me to a continuation school called Willow Park and they let me enroll no problem because I had a copy of my unofficial. They said they would need the official by graduation. I only needed my core senior classes. I went through those classes with ease. My fine bad boy and his family supported me all the way.

After so long they were my family and blood couldn't make us any closer. My relationship with mom was like the one that I always dreamed of. I had a little sister but I hadn't seen her since her grandma got her out of the system. But now I had two little sisters and two little brothers. The joy, happiness, and fulfillment were unexplainable.

Graduation quickly approached and I reached out to my dad. Not only did he attend my graduation but he bought me a car as a gift as well. The only downfall was it was a stick shift and I had no idea how to drive it. My fine bad boy, my first love, knew how to drive it. He mainly drove us around anyway.

There was a crack in the windshield and we got pulled over. Our little brother had a cap gun in his pocket and that violated my first love because he was on probation. I watched them handcuffed him and put him in the back seat of the car and drove off. I instantly broke down. I cried so hard it took a little while for me to be able to see clearly. I had a few lessons of driving the car, but I hadn't mastered driving the car yet, so the drive to uncle's house was a lot of stop and go.

I went to the court, talked to the police, and the probation officer. I was at court and they said he violated his probation and sent him to prison. My whole world fell apart. *Why? I was finally loved and it had to be snatched away from me.* When I was younger, I used to get on the bus and go to church just to get away. I never really prayed before that day. I drove and parked in an empty lot close to the apartment, cried, prayed, and screamed hitting the steering wheel. I just kept asking God *why? What did I do? Why couldn't he allow me to be loved? Why did He keep taking it away from me?*

I had mastered hiding pain, so I went to the gas station bathroom, cleaned my face, and went home to mom and the family with strength on my face but not in my heart. I wrote fine bad boy every day and he would call me but it wasn't the same. I missed his touch, smell, love, and presence. I went from feeling like I could conquer the world with him to feeling like I was nothing without him.

I thought it couldn't get any worse but that's when I got his letter breaking up with me. I was so distraught that I couldn't read the whole letter. When I got to the part of the letter stating, "I don't want you to waste your life waiting on me so I'm breaking up with you." I couldn't read the rest. I couldn't take it. I hopped in my car and drove to the parking lot. I drove as fast as I could. It was time to end it all, if he couldn't love me no one could. I was driving as fast as I could to a brick wall and I guess it was God because right before I hit it my car completely cut off. My bumper kissed the brick wall.

I got out of the car and fell to my knees. I cried out to God and said *why won't you just let me die? You won't let anyone love me. Why do you want me to suffer in this world? Why do you hate me so much?* I just laid on the pavement for a while and then I eventually went home. On my way home, I kind of chuckled because I knew God made the car cut off and then let it work for me to get home.

I tried so hard to act like I was okay. But mom could see through it. She always assured me that she loved me and she wanted me to be happy with or without her son. She encouraged me to date but I couldn't. In my heart I knew one day he would love me again. In my alone time I couldn't take the pain any longer. I needed a release so I cut my inner thigh. The pain of the cut felt so good it gave me such a release. It was just what I needed in order to get me through for a little while.

Chapter 7
I Tried to be Normal

Right before my first love got out of prison, he wrote me a letter. Mom called and I had her meet me at my job to bring it to me. I read the letter and immediately broke down and started crying. He loved me and missed me and wanted to get back together when he got home. I was pregnant but mom didn't know. I always assumed she thought I was crying out of happiness from the letter. But really, I was crying because I was pregnant with Levi's baby, but when my first love came home, I wanted to be with him.

I ended up losing Levi's baby before my first love got home. I was trying to purposely get pregnant at this point because I wanted what I had lost. The weird part was I never wanted kids until I lost that baby. Oddly enough my first love wasn't part of my plan. It's crazy how things actually happen. We hooked up a few times but my mind wouldn't register that the baby was his. My heart kept telling me but I didn't want to listen. I kept saying I live with Levi we are together basically every night it had to be his.

When I was pregnant with my oldest son. Levi and I got into an argument. About whether the baby was his or not and the things that he said to me. He was drunk and he swung me into the closet. He left after this and that unlovable feeling crept in again. I walked by Food 4 Less and I stood on the curb, I was in the middle of the sidewalk. I purposely waited for the light to turn green and the cars to start going. I tried to run out in front of the cars. They had to hit me. There was no way they couldn't, but God stepped in again. I was waiting for the impact but it never came.

I cried out again God *it's not enough that I can't be loved but now my son too? Why? Why? Why?* I walked back home. I didn't hear from Levi for three days. Then he finally texted me apologizing and saying how wrong he was, that it wasn't him, it was the alcohol. I should have left him alone then but I didn't want my son to be without his dad. Crazy part was the whole time Levi was right, my oldest son belonged to my first love.

My son was a few weeks old and I walked to Levi's mom's house. I was trying to get him to come home but he refused and we argued and he just kept saying my baby wasn't his and he was spending time with his real daughter. I was so hurt but knowing what I know now I guess I deserved it. At the time though I didn't know. We were passing this little bridge thing and I got up on it holding my baby ready to jump. I believed God spoke to me before but that time I heard him loud and clear. I will never leave you nor forsake you. I broke down crying and I walked home.

When we got home, I held my son so close and I apologized to him. I told him that no matter what, I would always be there for him, and I would always love him even if no one else did. I told him that it would always be me and him against the world and I would never leave him. He just looked at me and smiled for the first time and it warmed my heart and made me cry even more. It was as if he knew exactly what I was saying to him.

I was breastfeeding my oldest and I didn't have a period the doctor said that it was normal. I was at work trying to move a patient from the bed to their chair. I got dizzy and passed out, woke up in the emergency room, and I was pregnant again. I cried and cried; I was barely taking care of the baby that I had. He was barely accepted by his dad's family so why would I want to bring another kid into this hellhole.

I went home and told Levi and he wasn't happy at all. The first thing he said was get an abortion and I told him I wasn't killing my baby. I hoped and prayed it was a girl but nope it was another boy. Levi and I got into a huge fight because there were a rumor going around that his baby mama was pregnant again too.

I went off and he told me that I never gave him a chance to see if our family was going to work or not and I just started having babies. That I needed to get rid of it because he didn't want another baby, there was a loud bang at the door. It was his baby mama. *Are you serious?* I told him to tell her to stop coming to my house. He just got dressed and left with her like it was nothing and we weren't in the middle of a conversation.

I never wanted to have kids but it seemed like after I had my first son they were coming back-to-back. I tried every birth control method and nothing seemed to be working. It got to the point where I hated sex because as soon as I had sex, I was pregnant. I didn't believe in abortion but after baby number six, I was done.

I loved all of my boys. I prayed and prayed for a daughter but she never came. So, I finally came to terms with the fact that I wasn't meant to be a girl mom. The only thing was I barely knew how to be a mom at all. I tried my best to be the best mom but with all the drama with their dad and me not being responsible we were always hitting rock bottom.

I knew my sons deserved so much better then what I could actually give them. I was an orphan trying to be a mom and I was failing horribly. I got so stressed and so overwhelmed that I warmed up the iron and burned my arm twice. The smell of my skin burning gave me a sense of release. The pain was just what I needed in order to get through it.

Chapter 8
Simply Let Me Die

Inflicting harm on myself had become a drug to me. It gave me a high that I can't even explain in words. It was like my escape from reality, the pain was bitter sweet. It hurt enough to take my mind off of the pain I was going through in life, but it also felt good enough to give me the high that I needed, so in a sense, I lost touch with reality.

I was so lost in the world just trying to make it day by day. But the weird thing was I always found myself in church. Most of my sons went to preschool at church. I knew that God loved me but I was an empty lost soul. There were brief moments that I felt loved but there were many days that all I wanted to do was die.

My heart broke for my children because I was so lost and felt so unworthy of even being loved. I struggled giving them the pure and genuine love that they deserved. I was too busy fighting to be loved and accepted. I lost sight of being their mom. Going through the motions worked some days and others it simply wasn't enough.

Mentally, every day was a continuous battle. All I wanted to do was give up and die. But God on the other hand had plans for me and my life because I kept making it through day after day. Even the days that I begged Him, He always made a way to give me a little joy and a little hope.

I mastered looking, thriving, surviving, and living as if I was okay. When mentally, I was barely holding on by a string. It's a tough lesson to learn as an adult that the hardest part about life is to live when all you want to do is die. I just started to remind myself how selfish it would be if I killed myself and my sons were left without their mom. I couldn't inflict the same pain on them that I once felt all of my childhood. It never failed that when life was starting to smooth out and I would experience some joy. Something devastating would happen and send me back to that dark place. Where all I wanted to do was die. Fighting to live every day soon became my norm. It got to the point where every morning I would wake up and ask God to get me through the day. Before I went to bed, I would thank God for getting me through the day. This had become my morning and nightly routine.

Jeremiah 1:5 states, *"Before I formed you in the womb, I knew you."* He knows the plans and the purpose that he has for our lives. The enemy knows the anointing as well, that is why he tries to take us out at such a young age. My battle began when I was seven years old. There have been many days I just wanted to die, and many nights that I prayed I wouldn't wake up. But it took many years for me to realize my pain and my struggle was because I was a survivor. I had to overcome and let other believers know not to give up. If He did it for me than He can do it for them. God gave us life to live abundantly. That we shall live and not die. Many years, and days of my life I wanted to die but I thank God that He didn't allow me to die.

Chapter 9
I Thought I was Healed

The day that I received my divorce papers, I was so happy it was finally over. Now don't get me wrong I still loved him, but we had become too toxic with each other. We brought out the worst in each other and it was affecting the kids so it was time to let it go. I hadn't tried to kill myself since the divorce was finalized.

The separation from him wasn't what triggered a suicide attempt, because I knew it was necessary for all of us. It was that night when I was alone in my room and the enemy crept in. He reminded me that I was a failure, that I couldn't even be a good enough wife so my children had lost their father. That nothing had changed, no one could ever really love me, and if they did, all God did was remove them.

After drinking two bottles of wine, I went in the kitchen and grabbed the sharpest knife. I also got my pain pills out of the cabinet because I wasn't sure how I wanted to do it. I wrote notes to the police, giving them directions on what to do with my kids. I wrote notes to each one of my sons apologizing to them for my failure. Before I could finish the last note, my neighbor busted in my house. Again, God stopped me.

Fast forward to a year later, I married my first love and birthed a daughter. I published my first book, *Marrying Outside of God's Will*, created *Transparent Tuesday*, and launched *Crowning Queens*. In my eyes, life was perfect. The love that I once felt and was looking for again, I was getting it from my first love. I thought I was healed.

I was so happy, in love, and at peace that I made the mistake of letting my guard down. I wasn't on my praying post like I was supposed to be and that was when the enemy came in for the kill. I had my husband on a high pedestal and I was so in love. I didn't see any wrong in him. The way that he loved me and completed me, I was in total bliss. But God never allowed me to be caught off guard, I was asleep and I saw a person in our room in a whited T-shirt. My husband said I was screaming his name in my sleep. I didn't see a face, just the figure in a white T-shirt. That was my warning that there was a demon in our home. I prayed but I didn't take it seriously.

Not even a few days later my husband and I was arguing constantly. It wasn't normal for us. It was a sign in itself. The fatal day came and we got into it which led to him and my older two sons fighting. Later that day, my husband broke down and kept apologizing. It was like reality hit him and he honestly didn't know what he did. But the damage was done and war had begun between him and the boys. That day broke me because I'm his Queen and he would never do this to me. My savior had fallen from grace and I became numbed. I had to make sure my children were okay so I pushed my feelings aside.

The hate was in the house and no one was speaking to each other. It was as if we were all roommates. Another fatal day came and they got into it again. That was when the enemy almost took me out. I walked up to my husband and saw those familiar red eyes and I knew it wasn't my husband. Those same red eyes that were in Levi when he told me he would kill me the day I took the kids and left. That time I wasn't scared, I spoke boldly in my God given authority and told him that he had to go and he wasn't welcome in our home, that he had no authority and I was no longer scared of him. My mom sent me out of the garage.

I ran to the back yard bare foot; I fell face down in the dirt and cried so hard to God for my husband and my oldest son's soul. I stayed faced down crying and crying until I felt a shift. I heard my husband calling my name. I went inside the house. I looked at my mom and my husband and told them that I couldn't take the pain which was unbearable and I wanted to cut myself. Both of them told me I was stronger than that.

I was so broken I didn't sleep well. I would wait until everyone was asleep and go in the garage to cry until my husband came and get me. I would wake up crying and my husband would hold me tight and tell me it's going to be okay. I couldn't look at myself in the mirror. I couldn't shake the feeling of wanting to cut. My husband went out of town and I went to the tattoo shop. On one of my arms, I got tattooed all the boys' first initials with heart beats. On the other arm, I got tattooed my princess Genesis with heart beats. I didn't allow the enemy to win but I still needed that fix, so tattoos sufficed.

Everything the enemy intended for my bad God turned it into my favor. Over time my family healed and now our bond is stronger than ever. You would have never known anything happened. We don't look like what we've been through. No matter how good it gets, I don't come off of my praying post. And when God gives me warnings, I take them very seriously.

Chapter 10
There's Purpose in My Pain

When God gave me the dream of writing this book, in my dream I said, "God no not another book." I woke up and pulled up the google docs on my phone, I tried to play around with the title because it's hard on the ears to me. But God clearly said that is not what I showed you.

I didn't understand this assignment because I had been very transparent with my battles, and self-disclosed so much in my first book *Marrying Outside of God's Will*. Also, on Transparent Tuesdays, I am transparent with my weekly struggles and what I have learned. So, what was the need for the world to know that I really wanted to die? Why did I need to ask the world if they wanted to die? Now that I have sat and written this book, it wasn't partially for the world.

But for me to take a walk down memory lane and remember all of the times that I wanted to die, and God never left my side. To expose that cutting demon and let it know, you tried, but I didn't die. To remind myself not only has God brought me through the physical battles, but through His strength I overcame the mental battles as well.

I had to live to tell my testimony and to see the impossible become possible when I had my daughter. To know that I am worthy of genuinely being loved when I married my first love. The whole time my biological mother couldn't be the mother I needed her to be, she was battling her own demons. My mom/mother-in-law was my mom and with her I would have that mother daughter relationship that I always longed for. I also had to live to see my sons grow up and overcome their childhood and become intelligent, loving, caring, and inspiring young men.

So, on the days like today when mentally I am not okay, I am reminded of how far God has brought me. There is a need for my testimony during this pandemic because there are many like me who just want to die and has become a professional at hiding their pain and going behind closed doors begging God to simply let them die. This book was written to ask the question that some dare not to ask, give a glimpse of the times I begged to die, and realizing at the end all the reasons why we must

LIVE.

Chapter 11
How to Live and Not Die

The hardest thing about life is to live when all you want to do is die. Living not surviving, but actually living is going to take work and prayer. On a daily basis, ask God to get you through the day and once He does thank Him for getting you through that day. Also, I have 5 ways of how to live and not die. I do these things constantly so that I can live.

The first thing to do is **be honest with yourself**. But most importantly, figure out the reason for why you want to die. I wanted to die because I felt that I wasn't good enough to be loved. I was suffering because I couldn't find love and when I did, all they did was leave me.

Second, **be realistic.** No one's life is perfect and there are going to be good days, happy days, sad days, terrible days, days that you want to give up, days that you want to fight, days you want to die, and days you want to live.

Third, **constantly seek God's face.** Everyone is at a different pace in their relationship with God. But to live when all you want to do is die, God has to become your life line. There are going to be days that you want to give up, days you want to stay in bed all day and that is okay. These are the days that you need God the most.

Fourth, **remind yourself who God says that you are**. Create some *I am* statements, get some scriptures, and pick out five that works for you. Write each one on a separate sticky note and post them around your bathroom mirror. You will constantly have a reminder of who you are. These are my five.

Psalm 139:14... I am fearfully and wonderfully made. I remember this scripture when the abandonment thoughts creep in and I start to think that I am not good enough to be loved. Or the thoughts that after having kids I am ugly or that I have a big forehead.

Deuteronomy 28:13.... I am the head and not the tail. In life we all hit hard times, don't have enough money, homeless, or need a job. The struggles of life become very real, and sometimes very overwhelming. But no matter what the situation may look like at the moment remember you are the head and not the tail.

Deuteronomy 31:6.... I will never leave you nor forsake you. I have to be honest there are going to be some very lonely days in this life. Days where you feel as though you are the only person in this world. You may feel no one is on your side or has your back or no one understands what you are going through. That your back is up against the wall and you can't turn to anyone or depend on anyone. You also may feel like it's you against the world. This scripture is the most important one for me because when I start to feel any of these things, all I want to do is die. But I'll never forget when I heard God clearly say to me that He would never leave nor forsake me.

2 Corinthians 5:7... For we live by faith not by sight. I started to challenge myself to trust God, I mean trust God to the point that no matter how broken I was, homeless, jobless, didn't know how I would pay rent or even buy my diapers. When I simply have no hope that I will trust God. When I say trust Him, I mean no matter what is going on or how it may look I will trust Him and not give up. I started to tell myself these things. Easier said than done when you are looking at that eviction notice, when your kids are acting a plum fool, and it seems like you got more bills than money, and you don't know if your marriage is falling apart or not. Press in harder and walk by faith and not by sight.

There were a lot of days when I begged and pleaded God to give me a daughter and for someone to truly and genuinely love me. For many years I thought this was impossible because I kept having sons. The person that I was with and previously married to loved me but he didn't know how to love me. But we serve a God that makes the impossible possible. The life that I am living now I am constantly saying this verse in my head.

Psalm 37:4... Delight yourself in the Lord, and He will give you the desires of your heart. At first, I battled with this one because I was like Lord, I am delighting in you but you're not giving me the desires of my heart. The truth was I wasn't delighting in Him. I wasn't truly in the Word like I should have been, having a steady prayer life, or tithing like I was supposed to. When I actually started to do this my life started to lined up. I realized when I was praying for my daughter, I wasn't ready for her. My life wasn't ready for her. I was praying for pure and genuine love but I was self-destructing and self-sabotaging. I didn't know how to love nor did I know how to accept love. But when I delighted in God in His face and presence as well as trusting him, my life started to line up right which made it appropriate to finally have my daughter. I learned how to love myself, set standards for myself and how to properly love others, and that is when my first love came back to me. So, these are my favorite fives. I pray you create yours and post them on your bathroom mirror or any wall in your house.

The last but not least thing to do to live, **accept the things you cannot change and have the courage to change the things you can.** This took some maturing in myself, accepting what I could change and what I couldn't. I had to take responsibility for my actions and make some changes within my soul. I had to self-reflect and be honest with myself about my faults, what I needed to change, and how I needed to mature and become more Christ-like. Lastly, I had to stop blaming myself for things I had no control over and couldn't change. I had no control over the fact that my mom was fighting her own demons and couldn't be the mom that I needed her to be. I couldn't change that she was so hurt and felt like such a failure for losing her kids that she turned to drugs. I blamed myself for all of the wrong things that I had no control over, and wouldn't take responsibility for the things that I did do and what I needed to change. When my mom was in jail, she wrote me and said the following prayer would help me which was the Serenity Prayer.

God, grant me the serenity to accept the things I cannot change. The courage to change the things I can and the wisdom to know the difference.

This prayer became a game changer for me. This is how I live when all I want to do is die. Living is a choice and it is a constant battle. You have to choose to live and constantly do whatever it takes for you to live. My outline may be a little different than yours, because my battles are different than yours. But one thing we have in common is choosing to live.

Let's Connect

If my book has touched you and you seriously want to live. Know that you are not alone and I can help you. Please reach out to me I am also a Certified Life Coach. Together, we can come up with your outline to live and not die. You can email me at frances@crowningqueensllc.org

www.ingramcontent.com/pod-product-compliance
Lightning Source LLC
Chambersburg PA
CBHW071643040426
42452CB00009B/1744